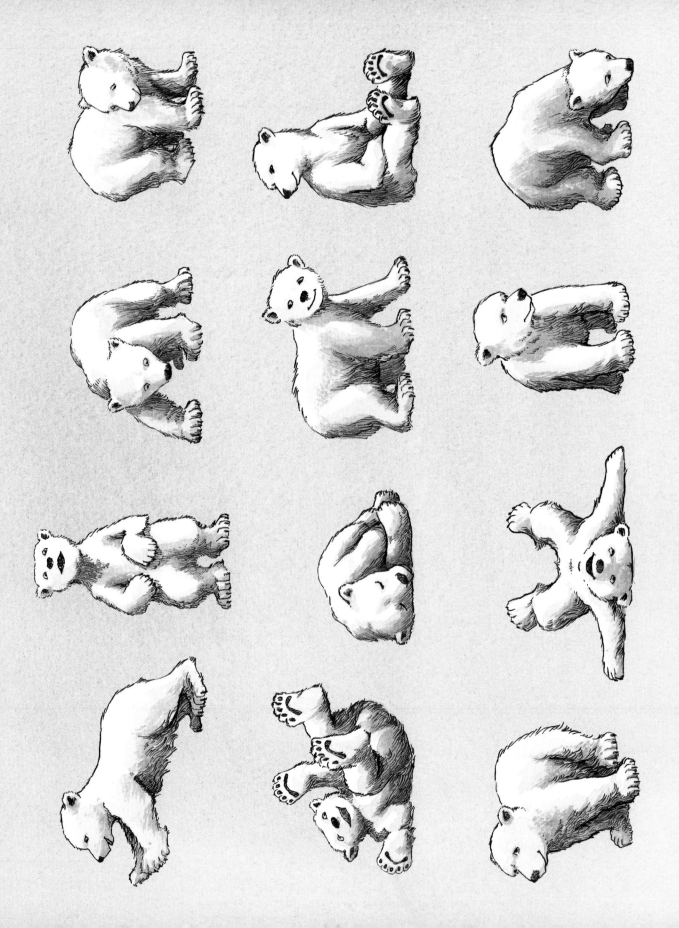

Where Do POLAR BEARS Live?

SARAH L. THOMSON ◆ ILLUSTRATED BY JASON CHIN

An Imprint of HarperCollinsPublishers

Collins

Special thanks to Mark A. Cane, G. Unger Vetlesen Professor
of Earth and Climate Sciences, Lamont-Doherty Earth Observatory
of Columbia University, for his valuable assistance.

To Jeff,
I owe you one.
—S.L.T.

For my grandparents
—J.C.

The Let's-Read-and-Find-Out Science book series was originated by Dr. Franklyn M. Branley, Astronomer Emeritus and former Chairman of the American Museum–Hayden Planetarium, and was formerly co-edited by him and Dr. Roma Gans, Professor Emeritus of Childhood Education, Teachers College, Columbia University. Text and illustrations for each of the books in the series are checked for accuracy by an expert in the relevant field. For more information about Let's-Read-and-Find-Out Science books, write to HarperCollins Children's Books, 195 Broadway, New York, NY 10007, or visit our website at www.letsreadandfindout.com.

Library of Congress Cataloging-in-Publication Data
Thomson, Sarah L.
  Where do polar bears live? / by Sarah L. Thomson ; illustrated by Jason Chin.
     p.   cm.
  ISBN 978-0-06-157547-4 (pbk.) — ISBN 978-0-06-157548-1 (trade bdg.)
  1. Polar bear—Juvenile literature.   2. Arctic regions—Juvenile literature.
I. Chin, Jason, ill.   II. Title.
QL737.C27T49   2010
599.786—dc22
                                                2008056030
                                                     CIP
                                                      AC

Typography by Sarah Hoy   19 20 SCP 10 9 8 7   ❖   First Edition

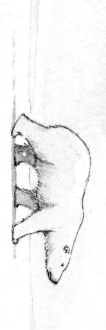

Where Do POLAR BEARS Live?

This island is covered with snow. No trees grow. Nothing has green leaves. The land is white as far as you can see.

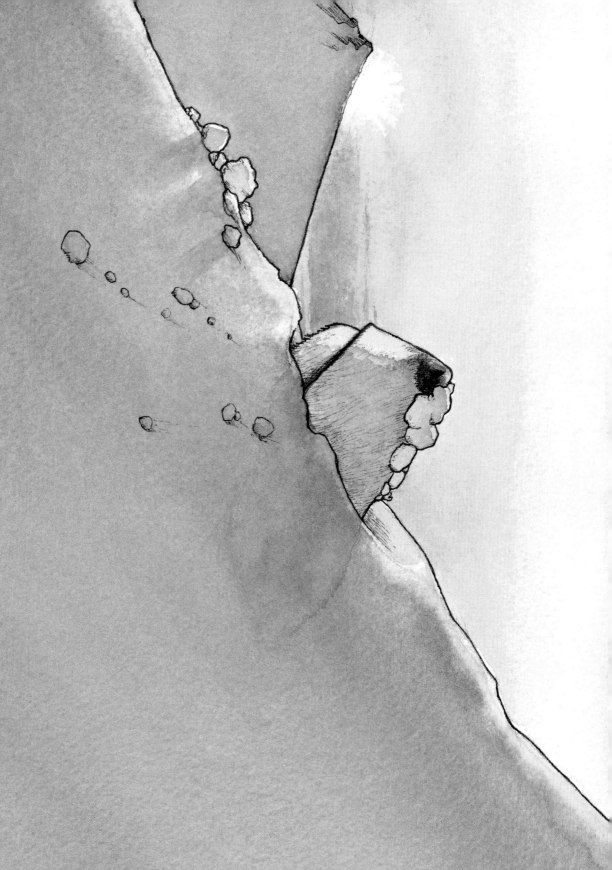

Then something small and round and black pokes up out of the snow.

A black nose sniffs the air. Then a smooth white head appears. A mother polar bear heaves herself out of her den.

A cub scrambles after her.

When the cub was born four months ago, he was no bigger than a guinea pig. Blind and helpless, he snuggled in his mother's fur. He drank her milk and grew, safe from the long Arctic winter.

Outside the den, on some days, it was fifty degrees below zero. From October to February, the sun never rose.

Now it's spring—even though snow still covers the land. The cub is about the size of a cocker spaniel. He's ready to leave the den. For the first time, he sees bright sunlight and feels the wind ruffle his fur.

14

The cub tumbles and slides down icy hills. His play makes him strong and teaches him to walk and run in snow.

Like his mother, the cub is
built to survive in the Arctic.
His white fur will grow to be
six inches thick—longer than
your hand. The skin beneath
the cub's fur is black. It soaks
up the heat of the sun. Under
the skin is a layer of fat. Like
a snug blanket, this blubber
keeps in the heat of the
bear's body.

Polar bears get too hot more easily than they get too cold. They stretch out on the ice to cool off.

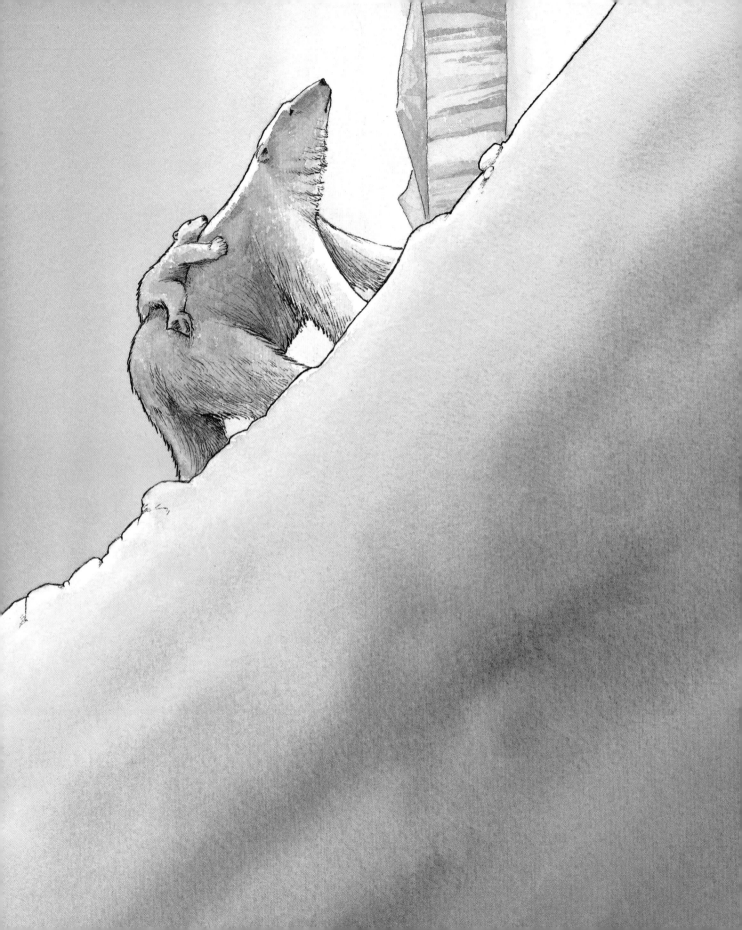

The cub has never seen his father. He never will. Polar bear fathers don't take care of cubs. For two years or a little longer, that will be the mother's job.

After a few days near the den, the mother leads her cub onto the frozen sea. Fur between the pads of their paws keeps them from slipping on the ice. If the cub gets tired, the mother gives him a ride.

Polar bears live in the Arctic, around the North Pole. Some of the Arctic is land. There are cold, rocky islands and stretches of tundra where no trees grow.

THE ARCTIC

NORTH POLE

But a lot of the Arctic is ice.

Under the ice, there is cold, dark water. Seals live here. So do the fish and shrimp and crabs that they eat.

Fish and shrimp and crabs spend their whole lives underwater. But seals have to come to the surface to breathe. They use the claws on their flippers to scrape away ice, making holes so they can reach the air.

23

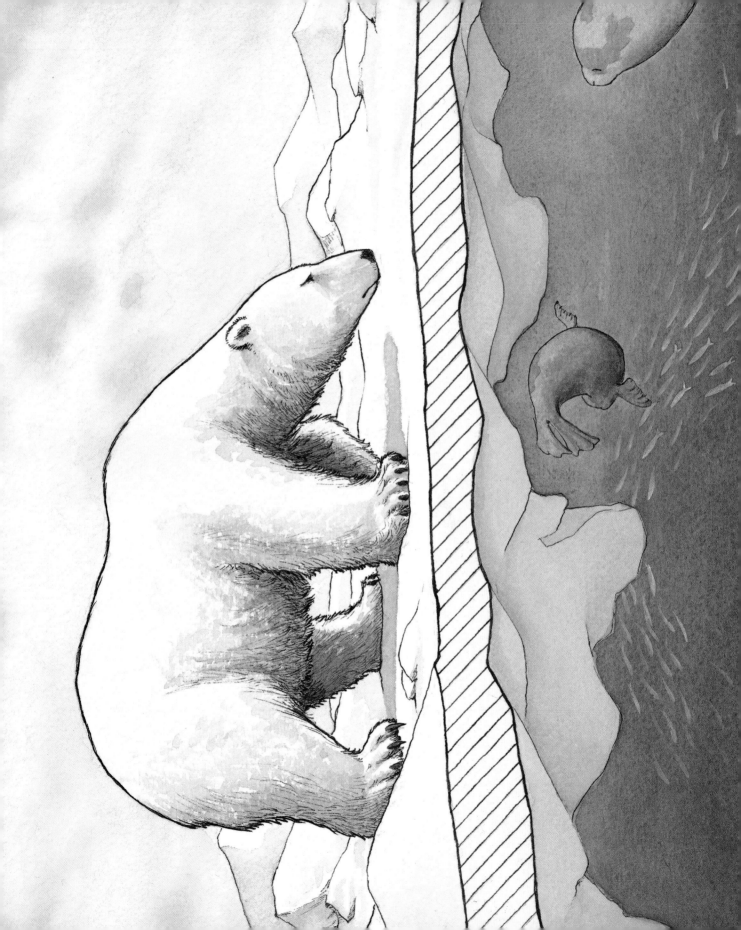

The mother polar bear did not eat for months while she was in her den. She has lost hundreds of pounds. Now she needs to hunt.

She smells a seal's breathing hole through three feet of snow and settles down to wait. She doesn't twitch a foot or take a step. If the seal hears the smallest sound, it will dart away to another hole.

At last, the bear smells the seal. She hooks it with her sharp claws and crushes its skull with her jaws. She drags it up onto the ice.

The mother strips away the skin and blubber. A little Arctic fox darts in to snatch a mouthful of the meat.

On land, a polar bear might catch a tiny lemming. It might even nibble grass or seaweed. But to survive, polar bears need to catch seals. To catch seals, they must hunt on the ice.

Every summer, some of the ice around the Arctic melts. Every winter, it freezes again. But in the last hundred years, the earth has gotten warmer. A little more ice melts each summer. Each winter, the water is slower to freeze back into ice.

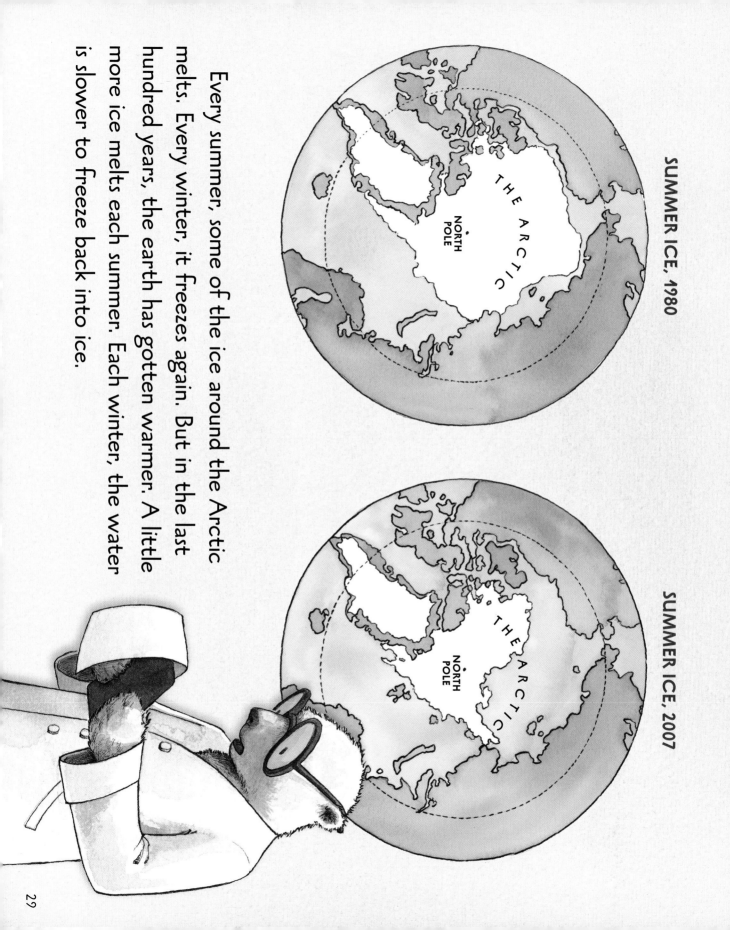

SUMMER ICE, 1980

THE ARCTIC

NORTH POLE

SUMMER ICE, 2007

THE ARCTIC

NORTH POLE

When ice melts earlier and water freezes later, bears have less time to hunt. They don't eat as many seals. When scientists studied polar bears in Canada, they found that the bears weighed less than they once did. Thinner bears can't have as many cubs. And more of their cubs die before they can grow up to have babies of their own.

If the earth keeps getting warmer, the summer ice in the Arctic could melt completely by the time you grow up.

31

When this polar bear cub is full grown, he will be the biggest hunter on land. If he stood on his hind legs, his head would brush the ceiling of your living room.

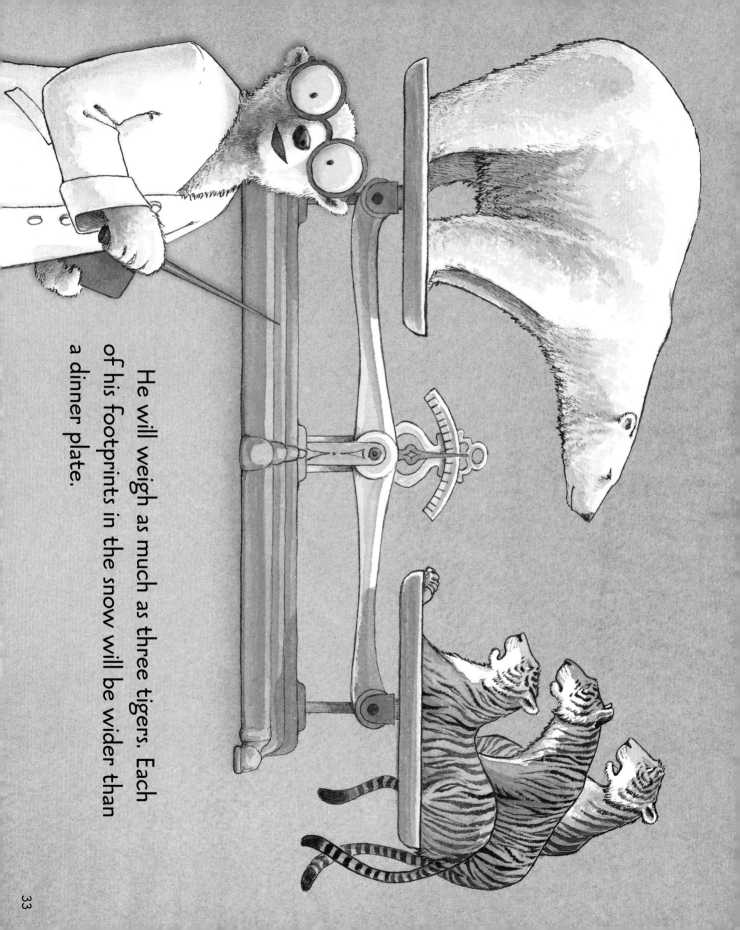

He will weigh as much as three tigers. Each of his footprints in the snow will be wider than a dinner plate.

This polar bear is a fierce, smart hunter. But he cannot survive with no place to hunt. Without ice, polar bears will become extinct—gone forever.

If the ice doesn't stop shrinking, he may be the last polar bear.

FIND OUT MORE ABOUT Why the World Is Getting Warmer

Our planet, Earth, is surrounded by a thick blanket of air—the atmosphere. The atmosphere is made of gases, such as the oxygen we need to breathe. There are other gases, too. One is called carbon dioxide.

Heat from the sun moves through the atmosphere to reach Earth. Some of it is reflected back into space, but some gets trapped by gases like carbon dioxide. It stays inside the atmosphere and helps warm up Earth.

There has always been carbon dioxide in the atmosphere. But when we burn gasoline, oil, natural gas, coal, and wood, we add more. The extra carbon dioxide is making Earth warmer.

In the last hundred years, Earth has gotten warmer by about 1.3° Fahrenheit (almost .75° Celsius). This doesn't sound like much. But even a small change in temperature can cause big changes on Earth. If we keep putting more carbon dioxide into the atmosphere, Earth will warm up by about 2°–11.5° Fahrenheit (1°–6.4° Celsius) in the next hundred years.

If that happens, a lot would change. In some places, there would be more rain and bigger storms. In others, there would be hardly any rain at all. Sea ice, where polar bears live, would melt more quickly. So would glaciers. Melting glaciers would make the oceans rise. Islands and land near the sea would be flooded. We're not sure what else might happen. But we know that many animals and people would find it hard to live if Earth changed so quickly.

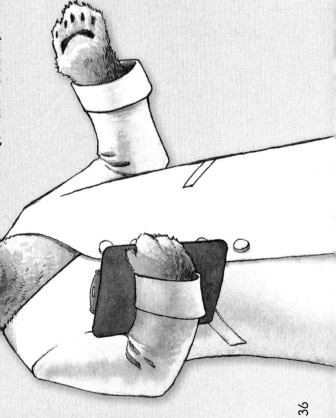

What Can You Do?

We put carbon dioxide in the atmosphere when we burn gasoline, oil, natural gas, coal, and wood. We use these fuels for a lot of things—for driving our cars, for heating our homes, and for making electricity. When you turn on a lightbulb, run an air conditioner, or work on a computer, you're using fuel that adds carbon dioxide to the air.

We can't stop doing all of these things. But here are some things we can do:

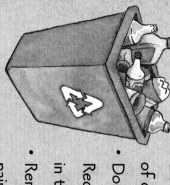

- Don't ask for a ride if you can walk or ride your bike. Taking the bus with lots of other people also uses less energy than driving a car.

- Don't throw soda cans, juice bottles, or paper in the garbage. Recycle them! Recycling uses less energy than making new things. That means less carbon dioxide in the air.

- Remember that paper has two sides. Don't waste it—use both! Draw or paint or write stories on the blank sides of old homework paper.

- Ask your mom or dad to buy compact fluorescent lightbulbs (the twisty kind) instead of the regular kind (called incandescent). They use less electricity. If your parents complain that the fluorescent ones are more expensive, explain that they will last much longer.

- In the winter, ask your parents to turn the thermostat down a little. If you're cold, put on a sweater or do some jumping jacks. Exercise warms you up.

- In the summer, don't turn on the air conditioner. Instead, sit by a fan (it uses less electricity), or better yet, an open window.

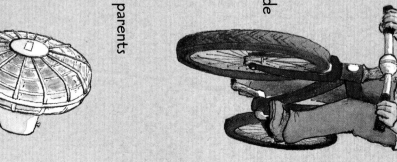

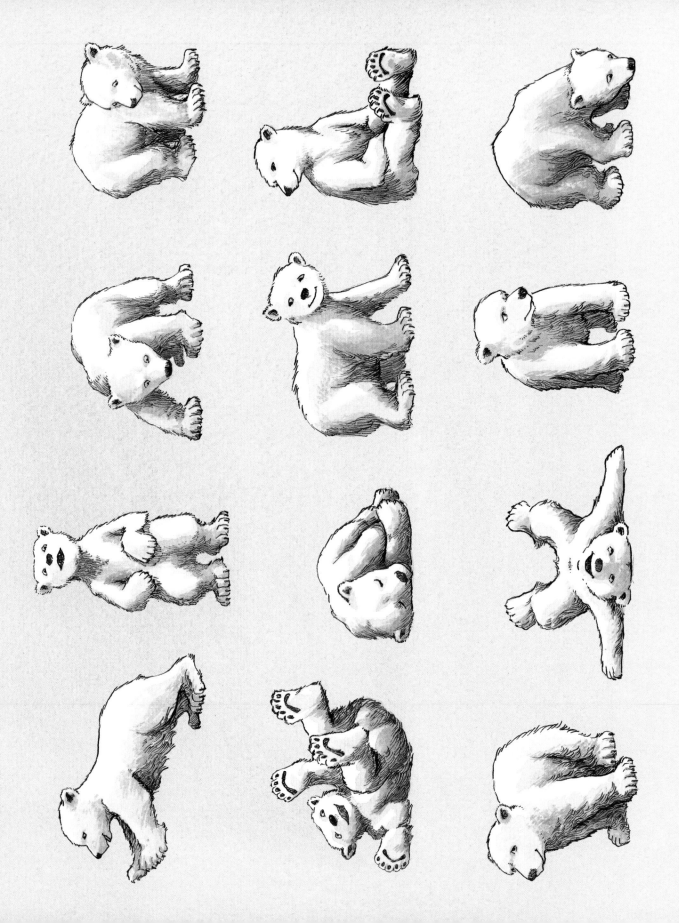